buck naked

is the opposite of hate

buck naked

is the opposite of hate

Poems

Joe Cottonwood

Sheila-Na-Gig Editions

buck naked is the opposite of hate © 2026 Joe Cottonwood
Cover art: Katie Col
Author photo: Ravi Malhotra

ISBN: 978-1-962405-60-7
Library of Congress Control Number: 2026934498

Sheila-Na-Gig Editions
Russell, KY
Hayley Mitchell Haugen, Editor
www.sheilanagigblog.com

Acknowledgments

My deep thanks go to these hard-working editors for providing first publication in their journals:

Sally Long, *Allegro*: "My Father, the Chemist"

Bryan R. Monte, *Amsterdam Quarterly*: "A shabby old woman," "Zoology: A Case Study"

James Diaz, *Anti-Heroin Chic*: "Chachoo," "If I see one more fucking Zen poem," "Last Time We See Bogey," "My Song Americana"

Sharon Smith and Marleen Roggow, *Birdland*: "Airplanes"

Dave Taylor, *Black Coffee Review*: "Bird Laundry"

Sandi Stromberg, *The Ekphrastic Review*: "Uncle Teaches How to Drive on Ice"

John Sheirer, *Freshwater*: "I've seen a thousand clowns," "I Was Raised by Birds"

Jeannie E. Roberts and Phillip Watts Brown, *Halfway Down the Stairs*: "Breast to Breast with Whom," "Crush," "Fixer-Upper"

Maryfrances Wagner, Gary Lechliter, and Greg Field, *I-70 Review*: "Tony Lamas"

Kew Gardens, London: "because a redwood grove"

Mark Ulysses, *Live Encounters*: "A feral calico cat"

Alan Catlin, *Misfit Magazine*: "Toast"

Dr. Jennifer Lagier Fellguth, *Monterey Poetry Review*: "One day There Was No Day"

Leslee Goodman, *MOON*: "Of Typewriters and Breasts, An Apology"

Zvi A. Sesling, *Muddy River Poetry Review*: "A Kitten, a Child, a Great Horned Owl"

Lori Desrosiers, *Naugatuck River Review*: "Mr. Hilton"

James Penha, *New Verse News*: "Children never shut the door"

Russell Streur, *Plum Tree Tavern*: "This is a poem about a full moon"

Roderick Bates, *Rat's Ass Review*: "Shirtless Dusty," "Summer of Love, 1967"

Irene Toh, *Red Wolf Journal*: "Lion Dreams"

Mary Crockett Hill, *Roanoke Review*: "My Wife Invites Her Ex-Boyfriend to Lunch"

Hayley Mitchell Haugen, *Sheila-Na-Gig online*: "All of your ancestors come to your wedding," "Anna's Hummingbird," "Juanita of Kansas," "Lester and Maggie and the 4-Wheel Bed," "Ode to Replacing a 50-Gallon Water Heater," "Private Parts, Private Thoughts," "Sika hires me," "Steak, Well-Done," "Steps to Closing the Cabin at Silver Lake," "The Stranger in the Car Behind," "Thin Ice," "Walter Johnson fires a fastball, Elvis Presley crowds the plate," "Welcome to the Woodshop," "We Should Show More Love for Bolts," "Working graveyard shift"

Melanie, *Silver Birch Press*: "Henrietta: A Summer Love," "Popcorn, Oil & Salt"

Andrea Janda, *Visitant*: "Eulogy, Old Pine," "Stick-Me-Tights"

Kusi Okamura, *The Wild Word*: "Ghost Dogs"

Rachel Barton, *Williwaw Journal*: "Open Range"

Lee Desrosiers, *Wordpeace*: "The Opposite of Hate"

Jayne Jaudon Ferrer, *Your Daily Poem*: "Kindred Spirits," "Little Frogs Are Hopping," "Pocket Pie," "Why is air? Why is a worm? Why why why?"

For Bobbie

Contents

In Muddy Water

Rough Cut

Swallowed by Lions

Let Go, Like a Dove

In Muddy Water

A feral calico cat

used to sleep in my truck like a ghost
leaving the driver's seat warm
but gone when I'd arrive.
Heard me, sharp ears.
Sometimes on the console
she left a bat with wings intact,
a baby rabbit, neck broken. Rent paid.
I set out kibble, she wouldn't touch.
Never bore kittens though I heard
nights of yowling, fights.
Later, her ears failed. I'd open the door,
she'd startle awake. Leap. Clawed
my shoulder once in her haste.
Near the end, she ate the kibble
but still got skinny, ribs outlined.
One day I found the food untouched. She'd vanished.
Like most animals, she knew how to die.

I tell you this because a while ago
in the garage, I found two children,
boy and girl curled together
in a filthy sleeping bag half under the truck.
On the girl, arms like wire. On the boy,
a scar like purple rope between ear and nose.
Eyes that hold fear and keep secrets.
I try to say *Estas a salvo aqui*—you are safe here.
They refuse to follow into *mi casa*.
Quickly in the house I grab fleece jackets,
a box of Cheerios, a jug of milk
plus bowls and spoons. I come back out.
Boy and girl are gone.

There's an underground railroad
of farmworkers up the coast of California
but my garage is off the main track.

An hour later, I'm loading corrugated drainpipe
when a frantic woman shows up. She's short, ragged,
missing one eye. Her language not Spanish, not English
but with fingers on her face she indicates the scar—
those were her kids. With a mother's super sense
she's tracking like a bloodhound.
All I can do is point to where they slept
and offer her some Cheerios, which she declines.
She takes the jackets. And then she's gone.

I return home after dark.
Running late that morning I'd left
the milk and Cheerios on a tool box.
Now nowhere in sight. Might've been an animal
except the bowls and spoons are upside down
on a smoothed-out shop rag, washed and dried.
Never see the kids or the one-eyed mom again.
Probably migrated north with the harvest.
This much I know: later, maybe a year,
one morning on the console of my truck
I find a jelly jar of wildflowers,
a paper bag of pears.

My Song Americana

I come to you barefoot
I chew bluegrass, drink corn
My rain is muddy water

My hands are raw from picking cotton
My lungs are black with coal
My farm is dust

I follow rivers by raft,
herd longhorns by horseback,
ride boxcars over endless plain

I killed the native and the buffalo
I regret
I sing of what remains

I am outlaw—I seek justice
I celebrate love—I betray it
I despise the rich—I want riches

I raise children in rags
They outgrow my front porch,
my tumbledown shack
I shame them with my twang,
my holler of blues

My children trade tractors for Teslas
They bring the south north
They take the west east

My children return with fresh children
who throw off shoes, who paddle kayaks,
who jump into muddy water
and come up clean

Tony Lamas

I buy a dump of a house in Frisco.
It comes with a tenant named Tito
who stays a few days trading work.

Tito spreads plastic on the steep roof
as a storm blows in from the Pacific. He's agile,
a daredevil in blasts of wind and splats of rain
as the sky turns black. Easier, Tito says,
than some sailboats he's crewed.

"I don't do good with kids," Tito says.
He has a child in Maine with cerebral palsy.
The mom, he says, started out gorgeous.
"I'm the snakebit type," he says. "I'm a bad star."
I tell him I don't believe in fortune and stars.
"Try sailing," Tito says.

Soon Tito departs, crewing to the Panama Canal
then up the coast, back to Maine.
"Kid's got my nose."
Traveling light, he gives me a pair of boots.
"I ain't the cowboy type," he says.

I find I'm not the city type. Sell the house,
go rural where my child Joshua finds
those Tony Lamas, too big for little legs
but he clomps merrily into the yard
only to be struck by a giant rattlesnake.

My heart screams.
Joshua literally jumps out of the boot.
The rattler can't extract fangs from the leather
and goes thrashing and dragging into the weeds.
Joshua unbitten.

Out there where the tumbleweed tumbles,
if you find by the light of stars a single Tony Lama
with a rattlesnake skeleton attached, take it.
Keep it. For good fortune.

Lester and Maggie and the 4-Wheel Bed

Gruff gray Lester and Navaho Maggie
have no offspring but treat me like one.
For Lester I knock down a wall
and install fat rubber wheels under
the walnut monster of a double bed
they've shared 60 years—so he can roll
Maggie to the dining room and kitchen.
Magpie of Dawn, Lester says.
She keeps an eye on me.
Maggie's delighted, room to room
joking and chattering sometimes in Navaho
and you get used to the scent of urine.

Rolling is difficult for Lester who limps
and later more cumbersome with oxygen tanks
so I'm replacing cupped floor boards
when Maggie who is watching me work
points to a pair of coyotes—
one large wary male, one smaller calm female—
outside the window sitting on haunches
by the broken-down tractor staring right at us,
not unusual for a ranch house outside town but
then we hear a gurgling sound like water in a drain.
Lester a big man leaps to Maggie's side.
Bends his head to her heart while outside
in broad daylight those coyotes start to howl.
The two. *Aroo-oo.*
It tingles.
The air itself seems to glow.
Lester grabs his rifle from the wall and runs
to the window but those coyotes don't flinch.
Aroo-oo.
He lowers the gun with shaky hands, says
They're calling her home.

A couple weeks later after the service
Lester in his old wedding suit tight and ragged
hands me a cardboard box containing the wheels
he's removed and there's a note:

> *For the next.*
> *Help them go home.*

Now I'm no coyote but that box is
on the top shelf in the garage.
I'm telling you, son, so you'll know.

Uncle Teaches How to Drive on Ice

Like falling in love, Uncle says.
Steer into the skid, not away.
Feather touch on the wheel.
Bridge freezes first but—Sammy frowns—
one time approaching the Snake River span
hidden ice not playing nice
sent his old pickup skating
so he steered into the slide, pumped the brakes
and stopped plumb at the canyon's edge.

Not far behind him
an AmeriGas delivery truck.

Even in a blizzard you can foresee events,
headlights through a veil of swirling flakes
so he bails from the old Ford face-first
into a snowbank just before a 16-ton tank
of liquified petroleum gas
like a giant hockey puck
plows through the pickup
down toward the Snake.

The cab submerges. Bubbles.

Soft the silence,
snow falling in sheets

and a woman appears
clawing up the embankment
spitting curses
ejected halfway down
fractured arm but she can climb.

She's a blue-black ponytail,
a white parka, red blood dripping,
she's an eagle with broken wing.

Says she's gonna sue somebody's ass
sure as her name is Sacajawea Jones and then
go home to Louisiana where it's warm
and purchase land down there.

Aunt Sac. Why her crooked arm.
Already on the black ice
Uncle Sammy's in love.

Walter Johnson fires a fastball,
Elvis Presley crowds the plate

At a tender age you learn to glaze windows
when you pitch tennis balls to the brick wall
of your house. You learn curveball and fast,
you try the knuckle, sweep glass.

You learn to hate the mulberries
that squish over the pitching mound.

You play next door with Mary Anne Morningstar
and you love the Elvis songs blaring
from her tinny transistor radio
as much as you hate the menacing hillbilly accent
of her full bourbon father who yodels
"Love me tay-ender, Love me troo-a-oo-a-oo."

You find you can improve your arm
only as far as your body will allow,
one fat pitch can erase ten good ones,
there's always some batter with a better eye,
some coach with a mean streak.

You learn your back yard was formerly
farmland owned by Walter Johnson,
one of the greatest pitchers of all time.
Your mulberries fed his chickens.
May his spirit feed your arm.

You develop hair down there
and see Mary Anne burst into tears
when you ask to see hers.
You jump back as she launches
a stone like a fastball into the radio
smashing it to jewels of plastic.

You learn she hates Elvis
and she hates her dad for his pelvis
and she loves God instead,
and you think maybe you love Mary Anne
like Elvis loves his momma
in a tender non-icky way.

You learn to cut glass, to curl putty with a knife.
You learn Walter Johnson after baseball
became an incompetent small time politician
and Elvis in Vegas turned squishy as mulberry.

You learn the easy passage from genius to fool.
Constellations fade with the dawn.
Remember Mary Anne.
Remember the stars.

Note: When Walter Johnson pitched for the Washington Senators he had a farm in Maryland. The house where I grew up was built on that farmland.

Working graveyard shift

my sleep is nuts
so on nights off I walk the dog at 3 a.m.
hoping a German shepherd normalizes me
except Quinn growls at the cop
who stays in his cruiser
talking through the open window
just letting me know somebody called
from one of those dark houses
but there's no law against walking at 3 a.m.
so have a good night.

Sometimes I jog the golf course under quiet stars.
I let Quinn off the leash.
Together we run over grass.
Even without a canine nose I love the smell,
the sound of sleeping snoring chlorophyll.

One night I'm running when the sprinklers start.
Immediately before I can think better
I pull off my clothes, every stitch.
I run. So free! It's fantastic, the dog agrees
until I trip
and roll
but that's fantastic too
except the bruises
and suddenly the spotlight, the cop.

I have mud on my body, grass in my hair.
The sprinklers keep chug-chug-chugging in circles
splat with cold bullets across my butt
as the cop writes out a ticket
for an unleashed dog. That's all,
because there's no law against
running through sprinklers
on graveyard shift
when you're white.

Juanita of Kansas

Road-tripping from goofy California
we are a mom, pop, 3 kids
come calling on Aunt Juanita
in calm Kansas this Sunday
surrounded by rustling rows of corn.
At a picnic table we eat barbecued
buffalo steak from Juanita's small herd,
Juanita's bloody butchering.
Tastes like spicy beef.

Joining us is one marvelous insect.
Gently it hovers, sets down on the table
like a puff of dandelion, size of a duck's egg
made of air and beams of light
with delicate spindly legs and
lichen-like scales of no apparent use
except beauty. Kids and I bend close
over the tabletop examining, exclaiming
"Oh wow," wondering what in the world
as if God's jewelry had dropped
from heaven until Juanita says
"I don't know what it is but—"
WHAP goes her big hand
and crushes the bug with her napkin.
"It's my farm," Juanita says,
and that's that.

Nov 22

My brother with dementia
outside a bakery arrested for peeing
into a newspaper rack and forgetting
to refasten his pants which brings him
not to a police station but a hospital
where I find him and take custody.
The nurse asks the standard questions
to see if he is oriented such as "Who is president?"
"That asshole."
"Which asshole?"
"Um—the ugly one."
"What year is it today?"
[Shrug.]
"What month is it?"
[Shrug.]
"Do you know what the day is?"
"No, what?"
"Today is Thursday, November twenty-second."
"They shot him."
"Who?"
"The president. They shot him."
The young nurse is puzzled.
"Kennedy," I explain.
"Well," says the nurse, "do you know where you are?"
"Yes," my brother says, "I'm in the fucking hospital."
The nurse smiles. "Okay, you may go."
"They shot him," he mutters all the way home.
Because some things you never forget.

Summer of Love, 1967

Here, this photo,
my cabin of teens in deep Missouri
after fathers beat, mothers abandoned.
No flowers in our hair.

Me in the center a college kid, clueless
with a summer job guiding hoodlums.
We canoed the Cuivre River.
I played guitar, sang folky stuff,
ate 23 prunes on a dare. They thought
I was a constipated Beatle.

Jayell caught frogs, built a fire,
fried the legs, shared them.
Oscar had an enormous penis, laughed at mine.
Little Roy caught moths, pinned them to an outhouse
wall where they fluttered and starved.
All had troubles. I loved all.

Where'd they go?
Three to Vietnam, this I know.
Jayell, Oscar, Little Roy,
names in a bathroom stall,
moths at a monument,
pinned on a wall.

Shirtless Dusty

I first meet Dusty on a beach
beside the Chesapeake Bay
in this photo where
he's dating my cousin Liz
who suddenly grew a body.
Dusty's the one with chest hair.
I'm the kid with glasses.

In this photo Vietnam shirtless again
he's on a river boat patrolling
writes *Stay in college.*
Stay the hell out of here.

Next here's him shirtless and Liz shirted
in the house he restored on steelworker's pay
building war machines that float.
Bankers stole his pension
when they looted Bethlehem Steel.
Combat memories haunt
while Dusty raises goats
until the city shuts him down.

Here's Dusty an old man on Facebook
with his face peeling off, flesh
flaking under cammo fatigues
posting paranoid gun-rights crap
so I unfriend him.

Here at the Chesapeake Bay again
Liz is dumping Dusty's ashes
from a borrowed sailboat.
Agent Orange kills him
though the doctors won't admit it.
His life like firing a rifle at the sky:
a disturbance the air closes over.

We open our shirts,
we feel the bullet strike.
Here. Right here.

The Opposite of Hate

Singin' in the shower.
Peanut butter. Daisies.
Weathered barn boards
are the opposite of hate.

Playmate. Roller skate.
Rhyme is the opposite of hate.

Balloons. The only thing
you should ever blow up
is a balloon.

Skinny-dips.
Swimmin' hole, hot afternoon.
Buck naked is the opposite of hate.

Steak, Well-Done

Selected on the hoof
after peering in the eye,
how Uncle Merrel shops for beef.
Walked by rope to an Amish man
who butchers, loads 500 pounds of meat
to Merrel's 2-wheel trailer pulled by
smoke-popping bare-bones tractor
to a freezer in town.

A few cuts Merrel brings home and cooks
special for us, his west coast nephew and family
who followed the Oregon Trail backwards
for dinner which is mid-afternoon
on farm country time in Missouri.
Back home we don't eat meat
but we don't mention.

Uncle Merrel is a patched old machine
pushed too hard for too long,
threads of flesh bound in scraps of denim.
Sweats red oil. Shakes when idle,
then at top speed he groans and grunts.

Steak, says Merrel, oughtn't be bloody inside,
you want it cooked but if you order well-done
in a restaurant they get mad at you
and flame it too fast so it's burned outside
but still bloody in the middle.

We appreciate we didn't have to evaluate
this steak in the eye. Uncle Merrel
cooks with time, with sizzling fat.
Well-done, still juicy but not bloody.
The farm way. And golly it's good.

The Stranger in the Car Behind

A mighty gust of fog rips 3 bicycles
from the rope-and-bungee web atop my van
to fly past the rear window as my gut drops
in a center lane on the Golden Gate Bridge
so I stop. God help me, I stop.

Jump out. Run back
to where the stranger in the car behind
blessedly not a tailgater braked in time
now has put on his blinkers and hustled forward
as together under steel cables
while wet wind howls with diesel smoke
as cars roar by on both sides
while an oil tanker glides beneath
he says not one word in the quick desperation
helps gather 3 bent bicycles from the roadway
which I stuff on top of 3 scared children
as the stranger to whom I said not one word
not a thank you not a moment for it
runs back to his car in the mad din of about 30 seconds
while I hop into the driver's seat
and stomp on the gas and — gone.

And the stranger whoever
never asked to be a hero
pumped adrenaline scrambled amid traffic
where no trucks or busses plowed into us
survived and drove on and — gone.

So to you right here right now reading this poem —
  Yes, *you* —
To all you strangers in all the cars behind
let me say in advance:
  Thank you.
Bless you for what without hesitation you will do.
  Thank you so much.

Rough Cut

Chachoo

Croaks like a crow,
scar on the throat like an implanted worm,
he's looking for work, for strictly cash.
Up north the season is short, labor is precious.
Everybody has nicknames.
I say we'll try you out, call you Chachoo for the voice.
Already got Petey with PTSD, Iggy the Inuit warrior.

First day Chachoo moves dirt, carries lumber.
Next day he's walking the top plate
balanced like a bird setting trusses, no fear.
Short, squat, strong as two men in one body.

Every noon a skinny girl brings
a hot salmon sandwich
and they sit together, quiet.
In sunshine his body sweats
like a cold glass of Coca Cola.
Any man tries to talk to the girl, eye contact,
Chachoo jumps in his face like a grizzly.

Friday before Labor Day, job done.
A dark cloud, cold wind. Could be snow.
Chachoo is tossing scraps in the dumpster,
final cleanup when the deputy's car pulls up front.
Warrant from Louisiana, name, photo.
Never heard of him, we say
because good work is good work.
A single leather glove, all they find.

A year later, in a warm city—hey!
Chachoo's daughter near the bus station.
I give her cash, tell her it's back pay, which it is.
"I'll see he gets it," she says.
"Did he really kill a man?"

Her eyes deep brown, so wet.
"He was protecting me."
I tell her: "All they found was his glove."
"He don't need it."
Then like Chachoo, she's gone.

In the back of my truck, under a toolbox,
sits that glove. Fingertips frayed, palm solid.
He don't need it. We all do.

Ode to Replacing a 50-Gallon Water Heater

Wrestling the mass of a gorilla
but less furry less flexible
removing crusty pipe
amid fragrance of rat droppings
and it is wet, puddles and streams of wet
because that is why you called me
so I bring the tools
the knowledge I carry
the pride

There is delicacy in plumbing
an art that rises beyond skill
to turn tight but not too
to thread tiny fittings
feathery fingertip to vise-like hand strength
to lift large
with visible results
a gleaming new tank

I bring warmth
to your morning face your dirty dishes
your strawberry shampoo hair
Think of me

We Should Show More Love for Bolts

I tell Roy he bought the wrong bolts.
Black iron, they'll rust in this forest, this rain.
We're building his cabin way out nowhere.
I build to last.
Roy returns to the tiny country store
where the hardware man laughs, says
Those bolts will be there
when you and I are long gone.

Building a trellis with my teenage son
who is my summer hired hand,
we are bolting posts to concrete anchors.
Placing a steel ring on a bolt I show the boy
how one side of the washer is dull, one smooth,
and I want him to place the shiny side out
even though the clients won't care
and in fact nobody will ever see
hidden by shrubbery and dust,
still I want the smooth side out because—
I know, Dad. He laughs.

After wildfire I return with Roy
down a washboard road through moonscape.
Roy is shaky, hair-trigger.
The cabin of 45 years is now smoldering debris.
We kick boots through rubble. *Look,* he points.
The bolts, still there. Roy grabs me in a bear hug
that lasts so long, holds so tight,
I wonder if he'll ever let go.

If I see one more fucking Zen poem

I will scream.
Enough with the footprints in moss,
the happy crickets.

I'm repairing a burst water pipe
next to a Buddha statue
on a McMansion lawn
in a soppy hole I've dug
as twilight darkens
while the client frets at my hourly expense,
tells me my fee is "unconscionable,"
he a psychoanalyst whose fee, no doubt,
has conscience.

The rising moon is my lover's breast
with shadowy crater her nipple,
those night clouds her fragrance,
the winking jet my desire,
the meteor my sperm.
As I solder copper pipe, boots in mud,
in this labor in my anger
I am strangely happy.

Welcome to the Woodshop

Young Kai at the age
when muscles grow quicker than caution
after his worst fuckup ever
shall spend a day in his father's woodshop
and they shall build an urn for Kai's future ashes
because Dad thinks it's time
for Kai to think ahead

First step, Kai, is to choose the tree
whose life ended to enclose
your dusty shadow

There's pine sweet as sugar, eagerly shaped,
easily injured by careless blow

There's oak so hard your enemies can't nail
but so resistant your teachers can't bend

There's acacia like a pretty dancer
with freckles dancing in curls of grain,
fickle to the chisel

There's walnut so dark
you want to touch and stroke,
disrespected by fools who seek the blond

There's redwood the pacifist
bending to gales, outliving fire,
outlasting dinosaurs, thriving in fog

Or there's bird's-eye maple
staring back at the life
you've sanded and shaped

From seeds to sawdust
what shape your grain, Kai?
What color your soul?

Fixer-Upper

Scraping moldy wallpaper
easily peeled
we find a message
scratched by pencil
on plaster:

Pleas love this house
where Babys grew
So much joy!
before sorrow
When spirits call
pleas give
our Blessing

Might spook buyers
lower the value
but *pleas…*
Over this spot
we place glass, a frame.
Not all flips are the same.

Sika hires me

to "shape up" her time capsule house
now that she's widowed from, she says,
"67 years of functional marriage."

Crusty pipes, knob-and-tube wires
eke out driblets of water and voltage.
I mustn't change the vibe, she says,
the blond wood soul of 1950s ranch house
because, Sika says, "Fifties was functional."

Sometimes, says Sika, she and Gino would argue
until they realized they weren't angry,
merely hungry, so together
they'd cook an omelette.

Sometimes in bed Sika would awaken
because Gino was thinking. She'd say
"Gino, stop thinking so I can sleep."

When Gino got snappy like a lobster
they'd drive an hour to the ocean
so he could wet his gills body-surfing
while Sika studied tide pools, and did I know
barnacles have a penis 8 times their body length
so they can reach their unknown neighbors?
If only people, she says, maybe sex
wouldn't be so damn awkward.

Sika's like a playful long-haired cat
unashamed to pause for licking private parts.

I tell Sika I need to open up walls.
Breaking eggs will be messy but when I'm done
the omelette will taste as great as you remember,
function in ways you will not see.
Sika says, "Precisely."

Stick-Me-Tights

Embraced by tarweed,
by clinging bedstraw and stinging nettle,
I harvest boards.
I'd rather embrace
the young bride who will scrape
a bungalow to build a mansion
but this old fence, precious like barn wood,
weathered yet strong, they'll use for decor,
perhaps the front door.

Decades ago
in a rougher town I set these posts,
nailed these planks for a prickly man
who leered at schoolgirls, offered massage.
A Molotov cocktail destroyed his garage.
So he hired me to wall the property
like a stockade for rusting Volvos
while the town grew less hardscrabble,
more gentry.

I speak no history to this innocent,
unborn when this saga began.
I am the ancient handyman.

She writes a check
while I pluck stick-me-tights
from shorts, from socks, from shirt.
Ick! she says. *Don't drop them in my dirt.*
So I've brought this handful of barbs
for you, my friend, the clutch of history
from weed country to do what seeds do.

Eulogy, Old Pine

One morning as I'm cursing a knothole,
a blast of wind opens the door.
Into the woodshop march six squirrels,
two doves, one screech owl
and a small army of purple caterpillars
(who eye the doves nervously but stand resolute).
That old pine fell for you, carpenter.
You are making shelves from our home.
Be worthy.
Or else what? I ask
but they're gone.
Wind bangs the door shut.

This pine in my hand feels warm.
My fingers, cold.
I am alone, myself and pieces
of a working class tree who did his job,
who gave shelter and took none,
who had an exterior rough, a personality prickly,
whose blood ran sticky,
who pleasured in sunshine and drank of rain,
who whistled in wind while bending with pain,
who gifted cones of careful craft,
who dressed yellow in fungus, emerald in moss,
who stood against bullying storm,
who donates his body,
whose spirit lingers
as powder on my fingers
smelling sweet as sugar.
Please may I be worthy.

Last Time We See Bogey

A three-tooth smile on a rattletrap bike,
refugee from a warm place fled to a cold one,
he sweeps sawdust, unloads bags of cement.

Pointing at the face printed on his T-shirt
he says *Hoom-fray Bah-gurt*
so we call him Bogey. Nearly deaf
except at the boom of a lumber drop
he ducks for cover, searches the sky.
Tremors, the hand.

Bogey brings a single mango for lunch, so we
"share." He loves bologna and peanut butter.
We give him steel-toed raggedy old boots.

Autumn comes fast with a sleet storm.
Kerosene heaters indoors (not safe)
hanging drywall when we hear a rattle outside.

Bogey's in an eggshell of ice
cracked at knees but frozen like glued
to the bike so we wheel him inside,
pour a thermos on gloves and boots,
then stand him dripping in front of the heater.

Jumping up and down trembling laughing
in a puddle of Guatemalan coffee he shouts
Cray-zee! You cray-zee! Won't let us
drive him home. Snot nose, body shaking
he cleans up scraps of drywall,
coughing at the gypsum dust.

Sleet ends, sunset is gorgeous,
color of passion and peace.
Bogey is shell-free, wobbling,
riding away with his small pay.
Not crazy. Gone.

Swallowed by Lions

All of your ancestors come to your wedding

By horse, by canoe they come
dressed in grass skirts and beaver pelt hats.
They bring amphorae of wine,
barrels of ancient beer.

They fight. Belch. Kiss both cheeks.
They hug too tight, make ribald jokes.
They embarrass you utterly.

They paint flowers on your face
and weave sunshine in your hair.

They smoke sacred herbs. Chant,
pound on drums, sing in lost language.
They puff music in hollowed bamboo,
dance in circles, juggle flaming torches.
They draw antelope on the walls of your cave.

As dowry they bring generations of struggle,
millenniums of sacrifice. They will come
to your wedding whether you invite them or not.

Wish them welcome.

Note: A few years ago, I attended a backyard wedding, a humble affair, a small gathering because the bride's parents and her entire family refused to attend. The groom was the wrong color, the wrong religion. He had worked for me briefly in construction until he realized he'd rather drive a truck. Bride and groom both had nothing in possessions— only love. When I looked into the defiant eyes of the bride taking her vows, I saw the spirits dancing there. In no way could her family boycott this wedding. You could sense them in the air. So I wrote this poem.

Breast to Breast with Whom

My job, maintenance on graveyard shift
so I'm up a stepladder at 3 a.m.
replacing ballasts in fluorescent fixtures.
A radio is spraying bubblegum pop
when suddenly some sober jackass
in newscaster voice is explaining why God
wants us to launch nuclear weapons.

This is it. I'll be vaporized
right here on this stepladder
in this godawful factory.

I want to jump in my car
speed to our cottage, to you,
to die breast to breast.

And then a kid about 18
with a push broom below me
sees the panic in my face up above
and laughs: "It's the crappy radio,
jumps stations. That's the God show.
You all right?"

I say "I just realized—It matters
where we die. And with whom."
The kid laughs, makes air quotes.
"'With whom,' Professor Handyman?"
Yes. With whom.

I remember this now
from bubblegum to Armageddon
as I say goodbye via Zoom to Aunt Nattie
all tubed up in a hospital bed, Covid,
closest we can come as her oxygen drops
with no one breast to breast.
She dies with whom?
Alone, with Zoom.

My Wife Invites Her Ex-Boyfriend to Lunch

She tells me Justin had good jokes,
good manners, was a card shark
and a militant Baptist. They broke up
because she always burst into giggles
when he kissed her. She never told him why.
Giggled, she tells me now, because
kissing Justin was like kissing a pug.

So we meet. Justin seems shocked
to see she's pregnant. Congratulates her. Us.
Justin has big lips and a fuzzy face.
Tells funny stories, has impeccable manners.
Says he's married to a woman who wants
to make films. Not movies. Films.
Says she has moods. Big moods. Says she
used to be political but couldn't choose sides.
Says she covered their new wallpaper with tinfoil.
Says she subconsciously converted their apartment
into a dump because that's what she was used to.
Says she's bad at choices.
Like, look, (he laughs) she chose *him*.

So, my wife asks, do you love her?
At once Justin and I are both on alert.
Yes, Justin says. Yes, we kiss. A lot.
That's good, my wife says.

After lunch,
we all shake hands.

Pocket Pie

The boy clambers
out of mother's arms
—nothing can stop him—
into my brand-new
fresh-in-the-driveway pickup,
seizes the steering wheel
and shouts *FWUCK!*
so we go for a spin.
Stop at mini-mart.
He points, asks, "Wha?"
I answer: "A pie that fits in your pocket.
Want one?"
Of course. Back home, parked,
we stay in the fwuck.
He turns the radio knob,
chooses rock. Classic rock.
I drink a beer. He bites crust, apple goo.
Saturday afternoon, April,
sweet as pie.

Airplanes

Trees grow craggy and cranky, says Noah.
One old oak grows sideways
so you can walk the trunk
and we do, Noah and me,
we walk up the tree and down again
balancing with our arms stretched out
like airplanes
which is cool if you're four
or seventy-four.

Noah decides to tour the drinking fountains
of Flood Park. Why not, this fine day?
So we run a circuit of twenty acres
with wings outspread, sampling.
Most fountains are concrete,
a few are shiny steel,
most in sun where the water comes hot,
a few under trees where the acorns fall.
One dribbles a bath for birds,
one blasts your nose.
Most of them paired—one high and one low
for the thirsty, for the curious,
for the very young or very old
with so much to discover.

Popcorn, Oil & Salt

In movie romance
you know the scene where one strips
(outer) clothes (this a television movie)
and jumps into water
(maybe off a cliff into an old quarry)
and then the other
(finding courage)
follows?

First some playful splashes,
then they tread water face-to-face
(droplets beading on brows)
and search eyes with caution, with wonder
(because in personality they seem opposites).

They kiss.
(Once, quickly.)
Now they check for reaction and
(if actors are good) we see emotions
play across faces from uncertainty to delight.
And they kiss again (slow lingering)
while the camera circles.

So I set down my bowl of olive-oiled popcorn
(Leccino makes it sweet, fruity, oddly grassy)
and say to you *We've never done that.*

You set down your of bowl of garlic-salty popcorn
(because you like it sharp, crisp) and say
Next summer at the lake.

After a moment of thought
(because you are you) you say
*How do they kiss and tread water at the same
time? Are they kicking super hard? Don't their feet*

collide? Quarry water is insanely cold. How does
the camera circle around them? On a boat? From
a crane? Oh sorry—were you about to kiss me?

And I say (with popcorn in my teeth)
Next summer at the lake.

I've seen a thousand clowns

pile out of a Volkswagen
but still I'm not prepared
when Amazon delivers a small brown box
and out pops a full-size woman
not the eye-candy type but the good-gardener type
wearing a tool belt packed with
puppies and flower pots.
I didn't order this, I say.
Let's get to work, she says.
On what? I say.
Exactly, she says. *You are so clueless.*
Give me some pliers, I say. *I'm good with tools.*
That's a start, she says. *Let's build a house.*
How many rooms? I say.
Kiss me quick, she says.
So I do. Not so quick.
Three point five bedrooms, she says. *For wee ones.*
While I hammer and saw, she watches.
And what will you be building? I ask.
Our relationship, she says.
I immediately invest every penny,
which isn't too many, in Amazon stock.

Twenty years pass.
It's worth a billion dollars, I say.
Give it away, she says.
But the children, I say.
Give it away, they say.
And I do.
Amazon sends an email asking
Were you satisfied with how the product was packaged?
Any damage? How did it go?
There are two checkboxes, *Yes* or *No.*

Zoology: A Case Study

See the soft soul
of one chiseled girl
in a vast city, Baltimore,
surreptitiously tipping books
to learn of ovary, sperm, egg,
singing in the Episcopal choir.

Her beauty is her enemy.
She escapes the choirmaster
to a public school staying late to peer
through the one and only microscope,
pursued by boys, men,
watching cells replicate, grow
feeling twin passion
a brain for science, a womb for womanhood.

A chance for university, scholarship
encouraged by a father of no education.
In the Great Depression she boards the train
for biology as a discovery, not a trap.

Sixteen years in St. Louis at a microscope
over *Drosophila* chromosomes,
a woman in a man's lab.
All the good men go to war.
A professor steals credit.

Half-starved, doctorate achieved,
Japan radioactive,
love unleashed,
last egg saved.
I'm born.

My Father, the Chemist

"Difference is the ionic bond of marriage"
said my father. Yes, he'd talk that way.
He meant disagreements, anger,
the electrostatic attraction
of oppositely charged ions.

Mom belted out *I don't wanna play in your yard*
or fingered a delicate *Moonlight Sonata*
while Dad couldn't sing *Happy Birthday*
except monotone. Deaf to music.

She died.
He conducted research in blood-clotting chemistry
so when his transient ischemic attacks began
he understood perfectly.
Told no one.

After, I found lab notes, self-observation
he'd jotted on a yellow pad with shaky hand:
TIA # 4 Date: 09/09/75 Time: 17:45
Music: $- / / ... / / - ... / / -$

Near death came music
which he scribbled as dashes and slashes and dots.
Then no scribbles for the fifth and final attack
but that night as he died alone in his bed
by moonlight surely she sang
Welcome, come play in my yard
and he heard, pulled to her bond.

Thin Ice

My daughter Lily asks why
I always buy plain chapstick
when she specifically asks for cherry—
Cherry, Dad!
I'm silent.

Carol's birthday, her 13th,
ice skating party on the C&O Canal.
I'm 12.
Carol has scars from a cleft lip.
Speech a little weird.
Her smile rare, one-sided, a sideways heart.
Laughter unknown.

Carol races me.
She's faster but stops with a shoosh.
I pass to the sound of crackling
like frozen bolts of lightning and I'm in water
like electric shock. My legs go through,
my torso flat on a breaking slab. Flailing
for a grip I reach Carol's hand.

Fingers touch, lock.
I clamber out saying "I'm okay
I'm not even cold" because I'm not yet
but my dad says "Take off your skates
and all that wet stuff. Undies, too."
I strip, Carol watching.
I've just grown hair.

By now I'm shivery, jumping up and down.
From the trunk of the Chevy
my dad finds a raggedy towel I can wrap.
We all wish Carol a happy birthday.
Her mom and dad kiss her cheeks,

then my mom and dad kiss her forehead,
so (towel like a skirt) missing signs
not knowing rules, I kiss the shiny red
heart-mouth.

Her eyes fly open.
Mine never close.
Sticky chapstick.
Her open hand presses the front of my skirt.
Firm hand. My entire body snaps to attention.
Her lips warm. Blood rushes. A new era—
with scent of cherry.
"Happy birthday," I say.
"Yeah," Carol says.

Years later I realize
she was trying to push me away.
Be careful with boys is what I should say
but "Sorry," is what I tell my daughter.
"Cherry," she says. "Next time, try to remember."

Of Typewriters and Breasts, an Apology

At the age of eleven,
in a brick school like a pizza oven
I took a typing class,
summer steamy Maryland,
then would practice at home bare top,
sometimes bare bottom in front of a fan.

At the age of eleven, a crush
can be crushing so when left-handed Ula
wild as a bobcat insisted typing is different
for a leftie, I said, "Show me."
As the fan rustled paper, as perspiration
dripped like grease from eyebrows, nose, chin
onto Underwood keys making Ula's fingers slip,
all I could think was freckles.
Dimple. Smile.

At the age of eleven, no matter the heat,
girls shouldn't be topless with boys
even with innocent intent.
We knew this. Maybe not so innocent.
Ula proved – yes – left-handed people
type differently. Or at least one did.

At the age of eleven, a boy
should not say aloud to a girl
that her little breasts look lopsided.
Left bigger, right smaller.

Both pretty, I might add at age seventy-one
were I ever to see you again, Ula,
and do you also, as I right now,
wonder what might have been?

Crush

Sharon in middle school floated as a cloud,
some days a fragrance like ferns unfurling,
others a wincing waft like bad hygiene.
I sure as hell wouldn't ask. Others would.
"Sorry," she'd say, her voice deep for a girl,
her eyes a flash of anger. No excuse,
no explanation. Kept to herself.

A pear-shaped body, a gorgeous smile. One day
in the library, the warble of a thrush startled me—
Sharon, her laughter over a book.
She had a boyfriend who was older, prep school.

Rode my Raleigh 3-speed the miles to her house.
From the wide street I stared at sunny windows,
white curtains until I felt stupid. Pedaled home.
"Did I see you on my street?" she asked next day.
"Yes." No excuse, no explanation.

Twenty-six years later like a bullet, sudden pain.
I fell down shouting AAGH. The ER doctor called it
epidemic pleurisy also known as Devil's Grip,
an infection surrounding the lungs and yes,
it comes fast and feels like it's crushing.
"Took your breath away, did it?"
Above the white coat her face, a fragrance
like ferns unfurling and I said "Hey! Remember me?"
The thrush laugh. A gorgeous smile.
Deep voice: "You were the quiet type,
so this should be easy. Just go home and rest."

Twenty-two more years pass and yesterday
out of the blue she messages me:
——**You okay? You keeping safe?**
No explanation, no excuse.

Some threads are invisible as virus.

I tell her I'm safe. Sheltering in place. What's up?

She's still ER, pandemic front line. She writes:

——**A surgeon died.**

A moment later:

——**My husband.**

I tell her I'm so sorry. How awful. How sad.

A minute passes. Then her final message:

——**I don't know what made me think of you.**

Lion Dreams

Harvey lurches, never walks.
His body is a puppet strung loose.
Can't hit a baseball to save his life.
Roger the bully calls him Special Spaz.

I like Harvey, like his questions
that teachers won't answer.
Questions like "If a lion eats you,
do you enter the lion's soul? And then
when the lion dreams, do you dream?"

Next time Roger calls him Special Spaz,
Harvey says "We're each special in our
own weird way. You're special, too."
"You calling me weird? Huh? You—"
That's when I get grade-school famous
for kicking Roger in the nuts. Which
makes me special in that weird way.

A few decades pass to now,
this grassy park overlooking the Pacific
a continent's width from Atlantic grade school.
I'm sitting on a black metal bench
eating a KFC drumstick. A man
beside me with short white beard,
white hair in a ponytail, tosses popcorn to
strutting doves and says "If you eat chicken,
do you swallow chicken soul?"

I gape, we laugh, we marvel at the meeting,
shake hands. His arm jerks at the elbow,
loose-jointed. Grip firm.
He says "I teach Theology at Long Beach."
I say "I fix houses. Rehab and restore."
"You remove the rot. Funny," he says, "how

we are what we are before we ever know.
All of us, from conception, we are
swallowed by lions."

Mr. Hilton

My Uber driver with bushy white beard
says *Wowza!* with a memorable pitch
not heard since high school as he
conveys me skillfully, rapidly
up and down the streets of San Francisco
so I say "Excuse me, but did you once
used to teach eleventh grade English
in Montgomery County, Maryland?"
For half a minute he grimaces, shakes his head.
Awkward, he says. *'Did you once used to.'*
Wowza!

In memory I drown. Speechless.
I'm the kid who doodled poems, stories for nobody
and for no purpose until clean-shaven Mr. Hilton
praised, encouraged, cheered.
Back then, he was gay and couldn't say.
Quoted Walt Whitman in a singsongy voice.
Sometimes he'd vow to quit teaching
and drive a taxi around D.C. and write
a novel about political mucketymucks.

"Did you write a novel?" I ask.
Drove taxi.
"And wrote a novel?"
Not exactly.
"You were my best teacher."
Thank you. He grins. *You just made my day.*

He studies me, eyes in mirror. *Who are you?*
I tell him my name and say, "You inspired me."
Inspired what?
I tell him I write poetry.
Sorry, he says. *A miserable occupation.*

The ride ends and I say, "You changed my life."
To be honest, he says, *I don't remember you.*
"Thank you for discovering me."
Nonsense. Wowza! You were always there.
He won't accept a tip.

Private Parts, Private Thoughts

Terry comes over for our Tuesday walk.
He bruised his leg pretty bad
going down some rocks on his motorcycle
so we don't climb any mountains today,
just walk the roads and talk about private parts,
the concept we impose on children
who are born without privacy
until we lay down the law at some point
for their safety, our comfort, society.

Terry was seventeen in Cincinnati,
she was fifteen and curious,
they shed privacy together
for an entire summer.
I remember skinny-dipping
on a sandbar of the Meramec River
in Missouri with friends,
private parts flopping, wet,
the same summer as Woodstock,
I guess it was something in the air at the time,
never expecting fifty-six years later
to be homeowners with SUVs,
old hippies with grandkids,
reminiscing. One of the Meramec girls,
Debbie, died in a car wreck a month after.
I still recall her breasts slick with the river,
upright, untasted.

We each are wearing broad-brim hats,
canvas sombrero for Terry,
funky fedora for me,
and we wonder about the lost custom
of tipping one's hat to a lady, so we try it,
tipping "Howdy ma'am"
and then simply "Ma'am"

like the laconic cowboys of old movies
as we arrive at the pond in the center of town.

Suddenly we both share a glance,
something in the air. Strip our clothes,
keep the hats on. Wade into the pond.
Cars drive by but nobody stops.
Fish, bullfrogs make way.
A great blue heron takes flight.
Squishy mud between our toes,
simply wading. Glory. Hot day.

Still wet, we pull our pants on.
A sheriff's deputy stops his cruiser,
leans, lowers the window,
says there was a complaint,
two old men naked in hats,
personally he doesn't care but
the young mothers seem the most upset,
what if the children saw?
"Haven't seen any," we say,
"but we'll keep a watch."
We tip our hats to the officer
and walk home with our private thoughts,
mine of greeting Debbie still a young lady
in heaven. Howdy, ma'am.

Let Go, Like a Dove

because a redwood grove

because naturally upon entering
     you lower your voice
because through branches on high
     fluffs of fog drift
     in shafts of sunlight
because you've met this feeling
     in cathedral, mosque, temple

because a redwood seems always
     to know what it's doing

because your body feels small
because your spirit grows large

because a redwood with its power
     will never preach
     makes no demands
     sips from the clouds
     swallows the sunlight
     shelters the chipmunk, the owl, you
because a redwood takes the long view

because the redwood withstands flame
     has kinship to stone, to river and earth
     to the patience of stars
     to the holy

because you forgot the question
     but a redwood grove
     is the answer

A shabby old woman

grows bristlecone pines
as house plants,
drops little seeds
into paper cups
with harsh soil
from Sierra mountainside.

Sunburnt seedlings frosted, parched,
she neglects for weeks fitting nature's plan,
her windowsill a forest growing
with the speed of centuries.

Her bedroom is cramped. Her love, prickly.
She remembers wooly mammoths,
survived asteroids. She gets angry
if you suggest orchids. The landlord
wants her out, wants to build condos,
turns up the heat.

In cups her love grows
for grandchildren to transplant
in faraway years, unfriendly soil,
to ever struggle, never thrive.
Please, may they survive.

Ghost Dogs

Ghosts of every dog
who ever owned you
fetch you from your bed
to lead you unleashed
through moonless forest.

Ghost dogs pause
to study scat of bobcat
blossom of possum
suit of love-struck newt.
Four-footed cannonballs
boom through brush
chasing a rabbit
who always escapes
and dogs ask with shiny eyes
Why won't you help?

Your senses elevated to canine pitch
you hear footsteps of spiders on the hunt
snores of squirrels cuddled in nests
heartbeat of snake
spooky silence of owl
as pant-pant-panting
tongue flap-flap-flapping
you gallop with spirits
who can smell your fatigue.

Yes they guide you home
they replenish your water
they pour kibbles of comfort
a bowl for your soul.
Unseen they curl on your bed.
Unconditional, they love you still.

Henrietta: A Summer Love

I do not claim to own this creek
but it flows through my property
and perhaps I own each day's gurgle
that wakes me, and beds me, alone
after a winter of slow goodbye.

Today, a new sound: splash and thrash.
A salmon the size of an otter
struggles upstream over gravel,
pool to pool where she rests, gathers strength
for the next leap and spurt
driven by a memory she does not remember.

Nine miles from the Pacific she stops
at this dark pool under my footbridge.
In a drought year, no farther. Henrietta,
I christen thee after my favorite aunt
who has your face.

I do not claim to own this fish
but all summer she hovers in shadow,
fins barely moving, facing upstream.
Water enters, water departs
too shallow each way for escape.

At the post office I happen to meet Debbie,
a biologist who knows salmon, who also knows loss.
Something compels me to bring her to my bridge.
A secret. In a town of anglers, we tell no one else.
Debbie says Henri is waiting for a lover.

Next day, and next, Debbie drops by.
I'm not sure why. Together, daily we watch.
Henrietta says little. Avoids eye contact.
Same with Debbie who says they often starve.
Waiting to spawn, they die.

One morning, October, I awake to the rush of rain.
I run to the bridge where Debbie is already waiting.
Her hand on my shoulder. Mine, hers.
Henrietta is gone.
Debbie says Henri might return next spring.
Please, she says, call me if and when.

I'm still waiting.
Strange, the signs we miss.
The love. The fish.

Note: The "I" of this poem is not me, but Henrietta is a true fish who made a summer rest stop in a pool beneath a bridge leading to a friend's house. Taking weekly walks with my friend I always paused to visit Henrietta. From such waters, the poem swam away and took on a life of its own.

This is a poem about a full moon

called a Hunter's Moon
I never saw rising because
I live in a valley covered in fog

Each night in a hot tub I soak,
each night a different phase of moon
before reaching my eyes
must scale the mountainside
to pierce the fog
with silver shafts
hovering among the redwood trees
like beams from a celestial projector.

This is a poem about a nose
touching my elbow
at the edge of the hot tub,
a black wet nose,
a raccoon cub wide-eyed with life,
handsome fur thick and glossy,
curious, electric, spirit of night.

Startled, delighted, I exclaim *There you are!*
like an idiot and the cub, scared,
so quick on its feet scampers—gone.

This is a poem about the felt,
sometimes seen, ever there:
fog, full moon, cub nose,
the damp touch
of the wild cosmos.

Little Frogs Are Hopping

Little frogs are hopping
from the pond to the weeds,
hopping in the headlight beams
across wet asphalt through strings of drizzle,
hopping where my car can only squash them
so I stop.

You take my hand.
"Thank you," you say.
You like frogs.

There is another route, an extra mile.
I back up, turn around.
"More cars will come," I say.
Again you take my hand.
"That's on them," you say.

We do what we can do.
And maybe, just maybe,
we spared a prince.

Open Range

You study me from the shotgun seat
making me squirm so I point to a cow
scratching her back against a telephone pole
with obvious bovine pleasure. Evening gives
Nevada a beauty it lacks when bright and hot.

We from foggy redwood coast of California
might never fit here but love passing
where somehow life makes a different sense.

One longhorn blocks us, ripping grass
from cracks in pavement. I stop the bug.
The beast outweighs it. We step out.

You're gazing at me, not the munching cow
or the oncoming night of white clouds,
charcoal sky in a silence made more so
by the chirping of a single cricket.

We're driving back roads to Boston
for jobs we don't want but ought to try
for career, for good sense in a stone cold city.

My bladder calls. Black-eyed Susans
line the road so I aim at rocks
as it would seem a crime to pee on flowers
especially with you watching as you are.

"I might be pregnant," you say. Your face,
always lit, now by starlight brighter still.
No breeze and yet the telephone wires
are singing, ringing.

Across the sky comes an orange flare,
too fast for a jet. I have time to say "Look!"

Without a sound the meteor explodes,
red fragments dropping like stars toward earth.

"I sort of knew," I say. The moon is rising
from behind a mountain silhouetting each pine.
The glow advances tree to tree along the ridge
like the hand of a clock. And now we don't care
if that cow stays forever.

"Thank you, Lucy," you whisper toward the beast
who in truth has no name but an ear tag.
Without a word we W-turn the jam-packed beetle
forward, back, forward, back on the narrow lane
and drive westward, drive home.

Kindred Spirits

I give my daughter, age one
who can draw better than walk
a pad of Post-its,
the tiny ones.

She crayon-scribbles
strange designs
and peels from pad
to place on walls,
on books and boxes of cereal,
under the toothpaste tube,
inside boots.

A year later, moving out,
cleaning up,
behind the clothes dryer
I find a mouse nest
woven of grass, of dryer lint,
lined by her Post-its
gathered by mice
for their gallery
of delight.

Children never shut the door

unless they slam it.
Muddy-paw dogs run through the house.
A dove lost, confused, flaps against the skylight.
From the turkey in the oven we hear
spits and gurgles. No gobbles.

In broad daylight Uncle Olaf and Aunt Gerta
strip to skivvies and soak in the hot tub.
The children join them.
The dogs want. We say NO!
They ignore us and jump in.
Then out. Then shake.

Grampa and his girlfriend Jennifer arrive
on a two-seater bicycle from fifteen miles away.
Grampa is eighty and has no hair.
Jennifer hugs everybody, especially the dogs.
We smile. We bring towels.

Uncle Simon on a stepladder catches
the dove in a hanky. We all make calming
coo-coo-coo sounds as he carries it gently,
so gently outside. Opens the hanky.
The dove flies to the nearest tree. Clutches
a branch. Head-bobs toward us. Thankful.

Now let's hold hands around the table,
close our eyes. Squeeze (gently)
the hand you're holding.
Let go, like a dove.
Amen.

Bird Laundry

My preschool daughter
tells me she doesn't want to grow up.
She wants to grow down and be a bird.

I unload the dryer and dump warm laundry
over her worm-wriggling body on the bed
as the phone rings and it's Tai
who says he woke up this morning
beside Alicia who was dead
and he should have recognized her little fade-out
episodes as transient ischemic attacks
but it never occurred to him because she's only 34
and now Alicia's dead and what should he do?

He's in Jamaica; I'm in California
so there's not much I can offer
except to say I'm so sorry.
She was so wonderful.
What a shock.
I'm so very sorry.

And she with a sock tangled in her hair,
she who heard,
who sees water on my cheeks
says sometimes birds fly into glass windows
and bonk their beaks
and that's the bad part about birds.

Toast

On magnificent wings
a great blue heron in the golden dawn
glides to a stop
where power lines sag on steel poles
to a stop
on a silver thread of shine
to a stop
bringing velocity sideways swinging the line
to a stop
contacting the next line
to a stop
POP
and heron is no more.

Power out for two hours.
Toast untoasted. Eggs unfried. Coffee unbrewed.
It is our own fault, this inconvenience,
don't blame the bird. Your fault. Mine.
Our dollars bought this design.
Singed feathers float over the marsh,
a reminder, a memorial,
if we care to see.

A Kitten, a Child, a Great Horned Owl

As Oreo naps in a sunny patch
the great horned owl drops like a cruise missile
to snatch with explosion of wings.

Howling, rising toward the moon
Oreo with feline super strength lurches.
Breaks loose.

Falls like a fuzzy pineapple.
Snatches a branch in a redwood tree
high as an eight-story building.

Your child comes home. What do you tell her?
Swallow hard. Point to a fur-ball
clinging beyond ladder height, beyond help.

Set food at the base of the tree.
All through evening echo the child's
Here kitty kitty into dark forest.
Tuck her tears into bed and pillow.

At dawn, lucky you, awaken to
a scratching at bedroom screen.

Is love a choice, or born within?
Might this amazing child
choose the opposite of hate?

After quiet reflection
might she respect owls,
their silent flight, their grace?

Behold Oreo, full-grown.
See scars of talon holes on her shoulders.
Watch as daughter strokes a peaceful purring cat
who evermore sleeps under benches,
never on top.

Anna's Hummingbird

On this careless planet
little Jacob shouts *I found a bird!*

I warn Jacob not to touch.
I tell Jacob it's an Anna's Hummingbird.
Fluffed, huddled on gravel over tiny feet.
Jacob says *Anna's vibrating. She's cold.*

I tell Jacob a hummingbird heart
can beat a thousand times a minute.
Mine too.

Our kickball game forgotten.
Can't you do something?

I take off my shirt, slip it under like a gurney.
Anna flutters, makes faint peeping noises.
She's scared!

I carry shirt and bird to the carport, bunch the
fabric like a nest, place under a lamp for heat.
We're trying to help you, Anna.

She lies on her side, feet outstretched.
He who can never sit still, crouches.
Get warm, Anna.

I could tell him. I don't.
But I'm shivering, I want my shirt back.
Jacob whispers as if blowing into tiny lungs
Breathe, Anna!

Heat lamp glowing, tenderly he waits.
Our hearts are slowing, spirits growing.

One Day There Was No Day

One day there was no day.
No birds sang at dawn
because there was no dawn.
We walked our dogs by flashlight.

One day there was no sun.
Through smoky veils
we stared directly
at a floating tangerine.

One day there was no noon.
Owls hooted. Porch lights never dimmed.
Deer wandered the streets
blinking tears of soot.

One day there was no you, no me.
One day we were we.
Scared. Seeking touch.
Please. Hold my hand.

Steps to Closing the Cabin at Silver Lake

Remove palettes of dock still slimy
with summer, leave only a stub.
With friends toast the beefy sunset
from rare to well-done to salted with stars.
Walk friends up trail to cars, sidestep worried
glances, say you're fine, say goodbye.
Listen as loons beseech, locate,
gather their lovers. Be fine.

Awaken to half a gray moon in half a gray night.
Equinox. Fog. Half everything, dark.
Bury compost, burn burnables, drain the pipes.
Store the hummingbird feeder, all gone south.
Bike a final ride among hills once cleared
as dairy pastures, now reborn as deep woods,
maple to hemlock toppling old stone fences,
a century of Adirondack second growth.
Wonder if the heart has second growth.

Return by bike to the stub. Strip,
jump, gasp in bone-chill, swim briefly
as your penis shrinks to peanut,
as testicles try to re-enter your torso.

Dress warmly. Walk through a final inspection.
Linger next to a little glass jug
where she would leave wildflowers.
Watch as a bumblebee yellow and black
drops with a thump from the sky,
crawls the windowsill with fuzzy grit
seeking color, entry, warmth. Imagine
on ragged wings, you fly.

I Was Raised by Birds

First by robins
of rosy belly
who listen to earth
whose gain
is worm's loss.

I played among chickadees
each given a crown
of black or brown
sometimes chattering
upside down.

I heard wood thrush sing
lullabies of burbling brook
teaching metaphor
before I knew.

My guard was blue jay
shrieking spleen
who never spoke of love
who broke a wing tip diving,
driving from me
the hungry snake.

I was nudged by crow
who laughed, who told jokes
who pushed my butt as I grew
until at last
I flew.

Why is air? Why is a worm? Why why why?

Because air fills
where nothing is.

Because wind is air that is moving.
It pushes the clouds across the sky.

Because clouds are water floating in air.
The water falls as rain
and the earth becomes mud
and then worms come out and play.
Careful! Don't step on worms.

Because worms are alive. They eat earth.
They breathe air, drink water.

Because you make me explain
the simple poetry of everyday life.

Because life with you is my earth, water, sky.
Thank you for asking why.

We Thank the Logs

We thank the logs
    in our wood stove,
    glowing heat
    through the night.
We thank the candle's
    quiet flame
    on our table
    giving light.

Thank you, water, filling creeks
    from the sky, sweet rain.
Thank you, heart, steady beat
    blood to wash each vein.

We thank the bread
    scent of yeast
    freshly warm
    at the knife.
We thank the air
    from leaf green
    to our lungs
    for this life.

About the Author

Joe Cottonwood is a semi-retired contractor in the Santa Cruz Mountains of California. Often nominated for Pushcart or Best of the Net, his poems appear in hundreds of journals as well as on refrigerators, city buses, a nature trail, a billboard in Kew Gardens and on bottles of aroma therapy. He lives with his high school sweetheart under redwood trees among wagging tales and dog-eared pages.

Also by Joe Cottonwood

Novels for Grown-Ups
The Naked Computer, Famous Potatoes, Frank City (Goodbye),
and *Clear Heart*

Novels for Children and Grown-Ups
The Adventures of Boone Barnaby, Danny Ain't, Babcock,
Quake! and *Four Dog Riot*

Nonfiction
99 Jobs: Blood Sweat & Houses

Poetry
Son of a Poet, Foggy Dog: Poems of the Pacific Coast, and
Random Saints